Investigating
TRANSPORT

Selma Montford

YOUNG LIBRARY

Be Streetwise

**Towns are exciting places to explore, but they can be dangerous.
All detectives need to be properly briefed and equipped.**

Always tell an adult where you are going, how you are getting there, and when you expect to be back.

Wear a watch so you don't need to ask what the time is. Check opening times. Always let a parent know if you are delayed.

Take enough money for your return fare, and both change and a Phonecard for phone calls.

Don't talk to strangers. Before you go out, talk to an adult about who to ask for help in an emergency. (These may include police officers, traffic wardens, bus drivers, and post office, bank or station staff).

Keep your hand or foot against your belongings.

If you have a bicycle, learn how to use it safely.

Never play on building sites, on roads or on other people's property.

Try not to go out alone, and be home before dark.

Learn how to use a public phone, and how to make reverse charge and 999 calls.

Have an up-to-date map, and check transport timetables.

Never accept lifts or invitations into private buildings, even if you are very tired or lost.

Know the Green Cross Code. Read the Highway Code.

Always look where you are going. Don't walk along looking up at buildings, or step backwards into the road.

Never drop litter. Look for a bin or take it home with you.

Above all, use your common sense.

First published in 1993 by
YOUNG LIBRARY LTD
3 The Old Brushworks
56 Pickwick Road
Corsham, Wiltshire SN13 9BX

© Copyright 1993 text Selma Montford, drawings Jackie Batey
All rights reserved

ISBN 1 85429 030 4

Printed and bound in Hong Kong

Contents

Egg delivery cart in the early 1900s

Train in the early 1900s

Delivery lorry

Charabanc outing 1924

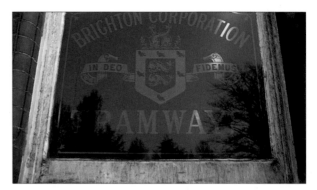

Tram shed converted into a bus garage

Bus in the 1930s

Canal narrow boat

Delivery van

Railway station

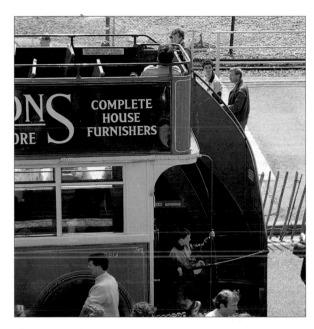

Open top bus

Taxis are public transport too

This car occupies a front garden

Mapping the Changes

Pathways, roads, canals, railways, airports, and motorways all affect the way towns have grown. The best way to observe this is to compare maps made before and after these transport routes were built.

Stations were usually built on the edge of towns, otherwise a lot of buildings would have had to be knocked down to make way for them. Most railways led to a dramatic increase in the population of the towns they served. Your local railway station is probably near the centre of the town, but it wasn't when it was built! The town has grown round it since.

Here are two maps, one drawn before, and one drawn after the railway was built. Look for evidence of changes which took place in this town.

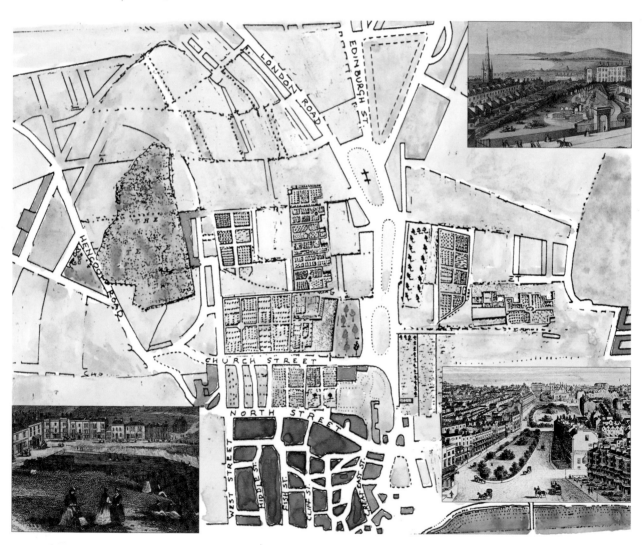

Many industries grew up round the railway, for example warehouses for house removal firms, furniture dealers, cab proprietors, cattle dealers, builders, coal merchants. Factories, foundries, and printers were set up near the station, using coal brought in on the railway.

Steam trains created a lot of dirt and noise. Houses built near the station were therefore mainly for poor families. Poor people could not afford to choose where they lived, or afford fares to travel to work. They had to live within walking distance of the factory or workshop. The railway enabled those better-off people, such as managers, bankers, and solicitors, to live further away from their work in an attractive area, up-wind of the factories.

Trains made seaside holidays and day-trips possible even for quite poor people. They created a tourist industry. Some seaside towns grew enormously in the nineteenth century, for example Blackpool, Brighton, and Torquay.

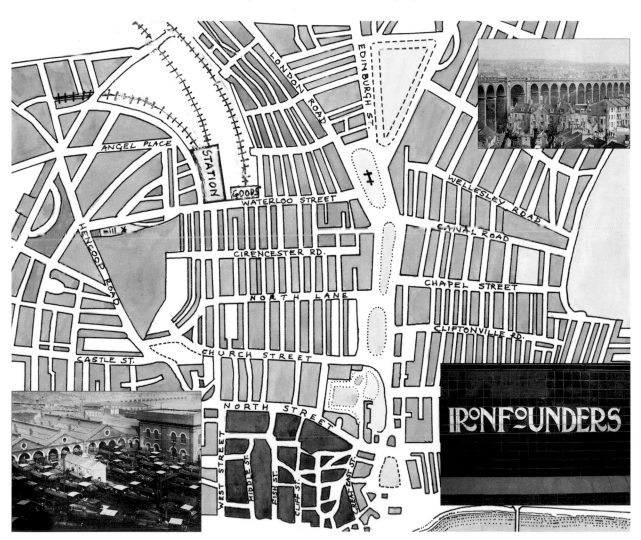

7

What's the Use?

The buildings on these pages were built for a particular purpose. It was something connected with transport. Some of them have a different use today, so you must look hard to find the evidence.

Sometimes only the name provides a clue. Railway Cottages, Station Approach or Viaduct Court, in places where you cannot see a railway, should make you suspicious. Some stations have been turned into restaurants or superstores after the railway line has been closed. Many mews buildings have been converted into smart cottages; others are now garages or workshops.

Coaching inns can be recognised by their arched entrance ways leading though to a paved yard. Perhaps the stables beyond have been changed into offices. A tram shelter may now be a bus shelter.

A tram shelter

The station below left has an engine shed built like a grand cathedral. Great iron arches support glass panes to let the light in but to keep the weather out. The roof is high so that there is plenty of space for the steam to escape into.

The railway running to this station has been closed. The station buildings are now a restaurant. You can eat your meal in the old ticket office, or in the waiting room, or even on the platform, when the weather is fine.

A coaching inn, with an archway leading to a paved yard surrounded by stables. The yard had to be big enough for the coaches to turn round. Coaching inns were placed every ten or twelve miles, for horses to be changed and passengers fed or rested. They were the service stations of the past

How many pubs can you find named after methods of transport?

Here are some examples

Horse & Groom	The Horn & Trumpet
Pedestrian Arms	Travellers Rest
Coach & Horses	The Ship
Station Arms	The Lock
Railway Tavern	Nag's Head
Bristol Flyer	The Packhorse
Bridge Inn	Pony & Trap
Farriers Arms	Three Horseshoes

Petrol station for refuelling

A tunnel entrance which is also a house

A railway carriage used as a house

A mews converted to houses

Waterborne

Before railways were built it was difficult to move heavy goods by road. In winter even main roads could be 20 or 30 cm deep in mud. Heavy loads were best carried on river barges or by coastal ships. Rivers were sometimes widened, straightened, or even deepened. But rivers only went where they wanted to go! People then thought about creating new waterways. They could then connect two rivers, or a river and a canal, or create ports far inland.

And so, in the eighteenth century, canals were built. They were a great success. Canals used to be called 'navigations'. The men who built them were called navigators - 'navvies' for short. That is why labourers today are still called navvies.

Canals were built to transport materials to factories, and manufactured goods from the factories to the places where they were needed. New factories and warehouses grew up near the canals, for the same reason that warehouses are built close to motorway junctions today.

Unlike roads, canals cannot run up hill. For short distances, hills could be cut or tunnelled. Dips could be embanked, or crossed with an aqueduct. Long hills were negotiated with locks. A lock is like a box of water with a gate at each end. After the barge enters the lock, the gate behind is closed. The water level in the lock is then raised or lowered to the level of the next stretch of water, and the gates in front are opened.

A lock enables boats on a canal or river to travel up or down hill

The Stretton Aqueduct, built of cast iron, was designed by the engineer Telford, in the nineteenth century. It carries the Shropshire Union Canal over the A5 trunk road in Staffordshire

The barge was towed on a long rope, pulled by a horse which walked on the towpath. Two people worked the narrow boat, one man to steer, the other to guide the horse. The early boatmen lived in cottages near the canal. As the canal system grew, the boats were built with cabins, and then the boatman's family did the work of the second boatman.

Fly boats carried passengers as well as goods. They travelled to a timetable at three miles an hour, day and night, using pairs of horses and teams of bargemen working a relay system.

There were passenger boats which catered for commuters and shoppers. On some longer routes passengers could book a night cabin.

But canals did not last long after the development of railways. A train could carry far more goods in much less time. Some of the railway companies bought up the canal companies, and then let the canals fall into disrepair so that the barges could not compete with trains.

Are there any canals in your area? They may be used for holiday boats now, or for fishing, or as a swimming pool, or for cycling and walking on the towpath.

Can you find one of the bridges which enabled the horse to cross the canal to the towpath on the other side?

Street Furniture

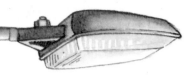

Street furniture can tell you a lot about the history and geography of your town. Which monarch's initials are on the post box? - it could be a clue to the date of the surrounding houses. The length of the bus shelter will indicate how busy the bus or tram route was when it was built. Horse troughs show that horses were used for carrying goods around the town. Some bus stop signs are made up of several numbered squares. How many bus companies are operating in your town?

Some traffic lights are hooded, some are topped with an electronic eye, some are computer controlled from somewhere else. Can you detect all three kinds?

LIGHTING THE WAY

Styles of street lighting may indicate the date of buildings. Can you see the ladder bar on old street lights? Whose ladder would have been propped against it? Why don't you see ladders propped against them now?

Ever seen any large guns in your street? No? Try looking at bollards, especially in port towns. Some bollards are made of old cannons, sometimes with a cannon ball fixed on top. Can you find any?

Bollards come in all sorts of shapes and sizes. See how many you can find.

Street Furniture

How many kinds of street furniture can you find in your town?
Here is a check list

Belisha beacons
traffic lights and their control boxes
British Telecom control boxes
pillar boxes
parking meters
tilt barriers
drainage and tree grates
drain, cable, and coal hole covers
monuments and statues
drinking fountains
bus stops
milestones
pumps and standpipes
telephone boxes and police boxes
bus and tram shelters
seats and benches
tethering posts and bollards
street lights
advertisement hoardings
plaques
street signs
railings and walls
horse troughs and mounting blocks
public lavatories

Can you think of any more?

Horse trough

DID YOU KNOW?
It is unlucky
to hang a horse
shoe upside down.
A horse shoe
holds the luck

Streetwise

Place all the counters on start. Throw the dice in turn. The person who throws the highest number starts.

Follow the instructions. The first person to reach 'Home' is the winner. You could design your own 'Streetwise' board?

For counters use small household objects, such as coins, a thimble, buttons, or a toothpaste tube top, a curtain ring or hook ...

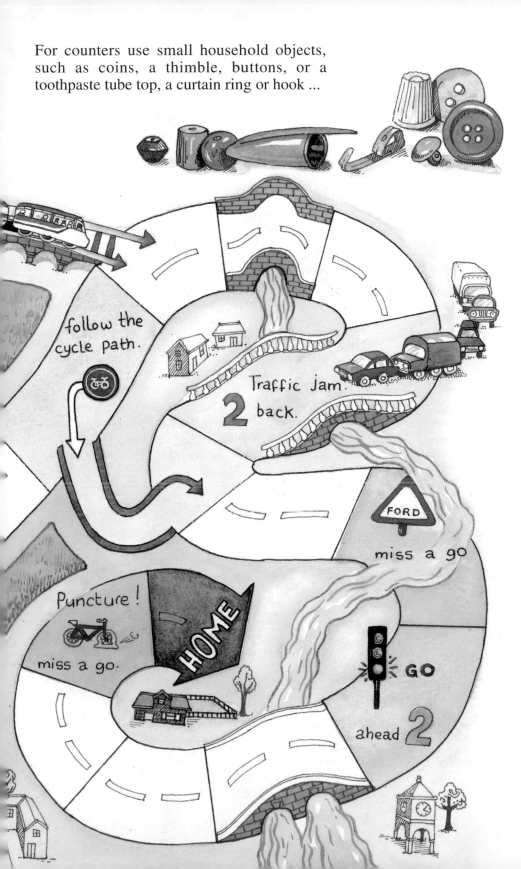

follow the cycle path.

Traffic jam. **2** back.

FORD

miss a go

Puncture!

miss a go.

HOME

GO

ahead **2**

Signs of the times. Do you know what they mean? Even the shape of the sign tells you whether it is a warning, a command or an action is forbidden. Do you know what these signs mean?

15

Train and Tram Travel

Horse drawn tramway in the 1900s

A tram in the early 1930s

The first trains were pulled by horses. Far greater weights can be pulled on rails than on roads, because there is less resistance between the wheel and the rail. Steam engines soon replaced horses, because they were so much stronger. The first steam railway opened between Stockton and Darlington in 1825.

Respectable people started to travel by train when kings and queens set an example. To avoid congested roads we need to encourage more people to travel by train. Who do you think should set a good example today?

Trains were the most important means of transport in the first half of this century. Unfortunately in the 1960s the government closed hundreds of small, under-used branch lines. They did not realise that the branch lines fed the main lines, or foresee what problems increased use of the motor car would bring. Buses were supposed to take the place of the trains, but bus services have now been cut too.

Who do you think has suffered most from the loss of railway branch lines? Who do you think suffered most from the increase in car traffic, particularly in town centres?

You may be able to find some derelict railway routes in your area. Start by looking at an up-to-date Ordnance Survey map, which marks routes of old railways. Look for evidence on the ground too: a station converted to another use, cottages called Railway Cottages, bridges with no roads leading to them, a level crossing gate abandoned in a hedge. Some old railway lines have been converted to walkways or cycle routes.

London's Metropolitan Railway was built in the 1860s, and was the capital's first underground line. It linked up some of London's main railway stations, King's Cross, Euston and Paddington, and continued to the Bank of England in the centre of the City.

The Thameslink railway line has provided a link between King's Cross, Blackfriars and London Bridge since the 1980s, as well as carrying passengers across London without the need to change trains.

Draw an underground railway

Which places in your town should be linked by an underground railway? You could draw the route on a street map.

Powering Along

Only a short time ago, before many people had cars, most people used buses, trams, and trolley-buses. Like trams, trolley buses took their power from overhead cables, but they did not run on rails.

Blackpool has kept its trams. If your town used to have trams it has probably lost them now. However you may be able to detect the old tram routes from some of the wide sweeping curves designed to allow the tram to get round the corner. Sometimes old tram shelters are still used as bus shelters.

The Docklands Light Railway

The Metro in Newcastle upon Tyne, and the Docklands Light Railway in London, are new light rail systems. Many people who are not willing to use buses seem to enjoy using trains or trams. Could you design a new bus which people would enjoy travelling in as much as a tram? Draw a bus shelter which is fun to wait in too.

> **Train spotting**
> Take a note book or palm top computer to your local railway station to record train numbers. You might like to take a timetable too, to check whether they are arriving and leaving on time.

Follow that Bus

The first buses (early nineteenth century) were pulled by horses. (So were trams.) Motor buses took over by the end of the last century.

Before the First World War most workers walked to work. Most town centres had a tram service in the 1920s. By the 1930s many people travelled to work on a corporation tram or bus. But reaching outlying estates, which grew up in the 1930s, was more convenient by bus. In some places the tram and the bus were combined into the trolley-bus – a bus powered by overhead lines.

A trolley-bus in the 1950s

Buses used to have a conductor to collect fares on the move. Then, to save money, the driver took the fares at the door, but this has made the service slower. Can you think of a better, faster way of collecting fares which allows the driver to concentrate on driving? On the Continent bus and tram fares are usually collected off the bus by selling tickets at shops and post offices, and from machines.

Design a bus timetable

In towns with many bus companies some bus stop signs are very confusing.

Could you design an information system for a bus stop so that a stranger to your town would know which bus to catch, where it was going, and at what times?

Conduct a survey

Conduct a survey of bus users. Ask lots of different people their chief difficulty in using buses, e.g. loading and storing their shopping, carrying their baby and push chair, managing the steps, standing in a moving bus.

Could you design a bus which made travelling easier and more enjoyable for all bus users, including disabled people?

Find out the cost of the journeys using different bus companies, whether you are eligible for special cut price tickets.

Design a bus shelter

Most bus shelters are awful, aren't they? Design your ideal bus shelter. Remember it must also be a safe place to wait, it should be vandal proof, and passengers need information.

Try sending your design to the local bus company. If they don't reply, write a letter for publication in the local paper.

Personal Transport

On horseback

Bubble car

Wheel chair and wheeled walking frame

The anatomy of a safe cyclist

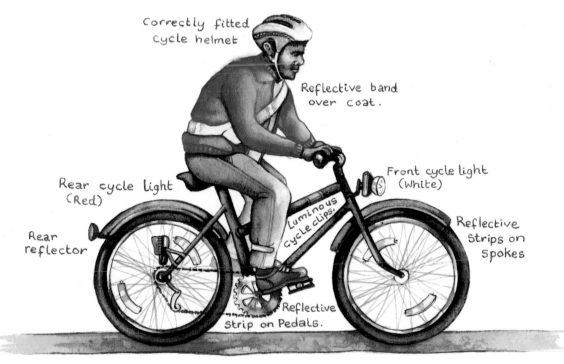

Correctly fitted cycle helmet

Reflective band over coat.

Rear cycle light (Red)

Front cycle light (White)

Rear reflector

Luminous cycle clips.

Reflective strips on spokes

Reflective strip on Pedals.

On the Road

First there were buildings, farms, castles, and villages. Roads came later, to link them. That is why most British roads are not straight.

No one wanted to pay for roads outside their own town, so in the seventeenth and eighteenth centuries they were financed by tolls. A toll was a charge made against every vehicle which used the road. Toll houses were built at the roadside. Whenever a vehicle or horseman approached, out came the toll keeper to collect his toll. They were about as popular as traffic wardens are today.

The sharp eyed detective will be able to spot toll houses, which sometimes project on to the road. Many still stand, and are now used for other purposes.

A toll house

Roads used to be little more than paths covered with stones. Now they are built with earth moving machinery, cranes, and prefabricated parts of bridges. Motorways are very expensive to build as parts are in deep cuttings, parts are built on stilts, and some have enormous interchanges which cover acres of land.

The first motorways were built in the 1960s. They were supposed to keep traffic away from the roads in towns, but the traffic increases to fill the new road space. Planners are now trying to persuade people to use their cars less, and to switch back to buses and trains.

All kinds of interesting machinery are used to maintain roads. The sharp-eyed urban detective should be able to see most of these during the year.

Street lamp repairs

Paving machine

Snow blower

Gutter cleaner

Pavement cleaner

Drain cleaner

Delivering the Goods

In late Victorian times, many middle class customers began to move away from town centres to the suburbs. The shopkeeper who wanted to keep his better-off customers had to deliver to them.

The individual grocer kept most of his customers in the 1930s, although he was losing some of them to co-ops and chain stores. The grocer concentrated on richer customers, who enjoyed and could afford the personal service.

Delivery rounds to outlying districts used to take all day, the shop assistant occasionally returning home at nine o'clock at night.

Whiteleys, a London department store, delivered to customers within a radius of 25 miles. They had depots at Croydon and Epsom and other places, where they kept over 300 horses.

Not many tradespeople deliver to their customers any more, and delivery vehicles are rare. How many do you know of? Sometimes a corner shop will put up a 'Back in 5 minutes' notice, while they deliver to an elderly or housebound person.

Your milkmen may also deliver groceries. Many milkmen have now bought the franchises of their rounds, which means they are working for themselves. They will be keen to tell you about the range of goods on their float.

Millions of people have milk delivered to the door, but how many know where it comes from? It could be interesting to find out.

A greengrocer's delivery lorry between the wars.

A milkman loading up his milk float before starting on his round

Some chemist shops will deliver medicines too, which is particularly helpful for sick people living alone. You might see meals on wheels being brought to an invalid.

You may be visited by mobile shops, or even a mobile library or clinic.

Follow the float

Where do they collect the milk from? Which dairy delivers your milk? What sort of vehicle collects it? Where is the farm which supplies it? What kind of cows live on the farm? Perhaps the farmer would let you see the cows being milked. You could discover which cow provided the milk for your breakfast cereal next day!

DID YOU KNOW?

That milkmen are an endangered species! Since 1970 their numbers have fallen from 40,000 to 30,000.

That the supermarket milk carton, is the reason for their decline? It is cheaper than the bottled milk delivered to your door. If you are out, it is not left on the doorstep.

England, Wales and Ireland are the only countries in Europe where there is a country-wide milk delivery service?

Whether there are any milkwomen in your town?

What time in the morning your milkman starts his round?

Sifting the Evidence

An urban detective looks for the evidence, and collects it in an orderly way. There are many different ways of storing information: computer, card index, scrapbook, ring binder, folder, audio or video tape, photo album, sketch book, or even a box or an old envelope.

The test of a good storage system is whether you can find what you are looking for easily. An even better test is whether another person can find what they are looking for.

Urban Studies Centres

Do you have a local urban studies centre?
This could be an excellent source of local information. People there will be keen to help you, and may be able to give you advice on how to organise your evidence.

Collecting old photographs and postcards

Be careful in storing photographs, which can easily be damaged.

Keep them dry, or they may stick together and be spoilt. Glue can discolour them, so do not stick them into a scrapbook.

Keep them in the dark, or they may fade. Colour prints can be stored in flip albums, negatives in special wallets, and both should be labelled and dated.

If you must write on the back of a photograph, use a very soft pencil, never ball-point pen, and do not press hard.

Model transport collection

Display your model cars, lorries, and other vehicles in a way that shows off their shape and the lettering on the side.

You could divide a shoe box into squares with pieces of card, so that one model stands in each square. You could use some of those large cooks' match boxes.

You may want to keep the model in its original packaging, which adds to its value in the future.

Museums and libraries

A local museum can be an excellent source of information, and may have local displays.

The local library will probably have a local history section.

Learn to use the index. It may be on a computer, on microfilm, or in a card index.

The librarians will help you to find what you are looking for.

That's the ticket

Every day we throw away pieces of paper which might have made an interesting collection.

Have you thought about collecting bus tickets, bus and train timetables, bottles and their labels, postcards, cuttings from the newspaper.

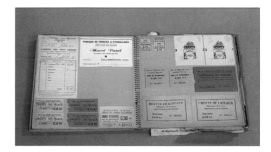

Many collections which are famous now were started by their owners when they were young.

Eye witness interviews

Practise using your tape recorder first. Try interviewing a member of your family or one of your friends. Grandparents will have many interesting stories to tell about their lives.

Start with a subject that you both know something about, such as school, games, or food. Make some notes before you begin the interview, and try to think of new questions while you are listening to the answers.

Ask questions which encourage the person you are interviewing to talk, rather than answering yes or no.

You could interview the lollipop person at your school. Not in the middle of the road!

You can start to build an oral history library.

You could play the tape you have made of one person to another person, to start them talking.

Remember to label the tapes and their boxes with the name, address and phone number of the person you have interviewed, and the date of the interview. Or, if you write or type the conversations afterwards, you can use the tape again.

Books to Read

Carrying British Mail, Jean Farrugia & Tony Gammons (National Postal Museum 1980)

English Life in the Nineteenth Century, Roger Hart (Wayland 1988)

From Manufacturing to Industry 1700-1850, John Robottom (Longman 1991)

How Towns Grow and Change, Laurie Bolwell & Cliff Lines (Wayland 1985)

Journeys, Rachel Bowles (Scholastic Publications 1991)

Population & Transport, Sue Warn (Arnold-Wheaton 1986)

Time and Motion, John Cockcroft (Collins Educational 1987)

Traffic Pollution, M Bright (Aladdin Books 1991)

Transport, Nigel Flynn (Wayland 1991)

Transport, editor Emma Foa (Hodder & Stoughton 1981)

Transport, Joanna Hughes & Rosemary Rodger (Ginn 1992)

Transport 1700-1850, John Robottom (Longman 1991)

Transport: the last hundred years, John Robottom (Longman 1992)

Transport on Land, Road & Rail, Eryl Davies (Franklin Watts 1992)

Travelling, Gill Tanner & Tim Wood (A & C Black 1992)

Village Heritage, Miss Pinnell (Alan Sutton 1986)

Acknowledgements

Series Consultant Jane Launchbury

Photographs Derek Pratt front cover, 11; Docklands Light Railway Limited front cover, 17; Tony McKendrick-Warden back cover (middle), 4 (top and middle left, top right), 16, 18 (left); Jane Launchbury 5 (top and middle right), 12 (middle & right), 22; Gillian Clements 5 (top left), 9 (top), 12 (middle), 13 (left), 22; Bob Seago 24 (middle), 25 (top right); Seeboard plc 20 (right); East Sussex County Council 21 (top and middle left). Remaining photographs Lewis Cohen Urban Studies Centre.

Artwork Jackie Batey

Maps Selma Montford 6; Lavender Jones 7.

Research Assistance Geoffrey Mead

Selma Montford is director of the Lewis Cohen Urban Studies Centre at the University of Brighton 68 Grand Parade Brighton BN2 2JY. It is an information, resource and research centre concerned with understanding the built environment.

There may be an Urban Studies Centre in your area; for a directory of Urban Studies Centres, Field Study Centres and other urban environmental centres contact the National Association for Urban Studies at the same address.

Index

A number in **bold** type means there is a picture